Spot the Steward

Written by Casey Elisha
Illustrated by Lhaiza Morena

Tate and his dad were going to Notting Hill Carnival. Shola asked if she could go too. She had never been to Carnival.

They took the Tube to Notting Hill. On the way, Tate's dad told them an important rule.

"If you cannot find me, look for a steward in a yellow vest. Stewards help people."

Tate's dad led them through the crowd.
"Let's find a good spot to see the parade," he said.

Tate and Shola were having lots of fun, but then ...

"Oh no!" cried Tate. "Where is Dad?" Tate's dad was not there!
"What shall we do?" Shola asked.

"Remember the rule!" Tate said. "We should find a steward."

"Where could they be?" asked Shola.

Shola could see stands selling yummy food.

"There might be a steward that way!" said Tate.

A big float went past. People had bright costumes. Flags flew in the sky.

Some people were playing big silver instruments.

"Those are called steel pans," Tate said.

Tate felt the beat. He began nodding along again but Shola reminded him …

"We have to find the steward!"

"Look!" Shola had spotted a yellow vest near a food stand.

Just as they were reaching the steward, a person called, "Tate! Shola!"

"Dad!" Tate shouted, and ran to him.
"We thought we were lost!" Shola said, following behind.

"I could see you all the time," Tate's dad said. "Good job following the rules!"

"Now we should have some fun!"